FROM ALBA͡ TO ZARA͡AN

A MONSTROUS A TO Z

words by
Matt Lake & K. Patrick Glover
pictures by
Tessa Mills

From Albatwitch to Zaratan

A parnilis media production
P.O. box 1461
Media, pa 19063

PREFACE

Every list of animals that you have ever heard

Includes the same few animals and we think that's absurd.

You've heard about gorillas, zebras, lions, and cats.

Of dogs and snakes and horses, birds and fish and bats.

So in this book

We'll take a look

At creatures, great and small

That you may not have heard of at any time at all.

And just to make matters a little bit worse

We've chosen to cover these creatures in verse.

Brace yourselves. Read on.

But play it safe: don't feed one.

A is for Albatwitch

The albatwitch is roaming 'round
In central Pennsylvania.
Who'd have thought this hallowed ground
Could actually sustain ya?

The small ape man this state adores
Lurks around in woods and bogs
Leaving trails of apple cores
Avoiding hikers and their dogs.

Albatwitch, what are you?
Are you ape or man?
Do you have a name we'd know—
like Frank or Fred or Betty?
Let us know, please, if you can,
You half-sized, small-foot yeti.

B is for Barghest

On the dales of Yorkshire, England,
Where fog obscures the night,
A large black hound with fiery eyes
Can make a strong man cower in fright.

It's a ghastly spectral vision
That the old ones call Barghest.
It haunts those northern lands
On some unholy quest.

And if you ever see the beast,
That is, if you survive,
Then tell your tale and add your voice,
So the legend stays alive.

C is for Cactus Cat

It slinks through the night in that hot barren place
It's up to no good with a smile on its face
It'll steal some of this and it'll stalk some of that
You better watch out for that slick cactus Cat

It'll slash at a cactus till its juices run out
Then it lets them ferment till they taste just like stout
It gets soused on its work, lickety-splat
You better watch out for that drunk cactus Cat

It sleeps through the day in a hollowed-out plant
And it hunts in the night with intent to enchant
It mesmerizes its prey just like that
You better watch out for that mean cactus Cat

But all your precautions will be just for naught
For all of your planning and all of your thought
And every attempt you make will fall flat
Because you'll never out think that sly cactus Cat

D is for Dover Demon

They call it a demon but there's no sulfur or brimstone,
And its skin wasn't red but more of a grey tone.
It didn't have horns, its head smooth as a dome,
But one thing is certain, he looked far from home.

It was long and thin and it seemed almost pale.
In fact, it seemed downright sickly and frail.
No one was frightened but only perplexed.
In truth quite a few were really quite vexed.

They all wanted a monster that would make Dover famous,
But this little critter was simply the tamest.
Of all the cryptozoological creatures among us,
The Demon ranks as one of the dullest.

E is for Elwetritsch

It used to be my fondest wish
To hunt and catch an Elwetritsch.
This birds stalks Germany's south-west
And Germans there all think it best
To let the strangers hunt this bird.
(They all think the hunt's absurd
For nobody has caught one yet
Though hundreds and hundreds have taken the bet.)

F is for the Flatwoods Monster

In the dark of the night, it fell from the sky.
It got to its feet and I tell you no lie,
It stood ten feet tall and had big glowing eyes.
We all thought at first it must be a disguise.

Its head was the shape of a playing card spade,
And it smelled like something come out of the grave.
It hissed as it moved and it moved in a glide,
And everyone ran or attempted to hide.

We never saw where it happened to go,
And it left not a trace in the new fallen snow,
Except that one mark out behind the old barn,
And in that lies the truth at the heart of this yarn.

It was burned into the ground, so it must have been hot,
And it was shaped like an unearthly thingamanot,
But if you held up a mirror and you looked thereupon,
You'd see written in clay it said made in Taiwan.

G is for Goatman

In Prince George's County
Down old Beltsville way
A creature broke out of a lab
And made those doctors pay!
They'd built him out of human and goatish DNA
And from that time the Goatman
Stalked the Governor's Bridge highway.
Go, go Goatman! Race those cars
And run them off the road.
Give those night-time drivers
An exciting episode.
Publicize their wicked science.
Make evildoers rue their pride.
Maryland's Godzilla (perhaps Goatzilla? You decide!)
Make those nasty scientists in Beltsville petrified.
For monster creation is really bad science
So from monsters we all should expect noncompliance.

H is for Hodag

The noble Hodag roams around
Through Wisconsin's fertile ground—
In Rhinelander, to be specific,
(Two thousand miles from the Pacific).
Seven feet long; three hundred pounds
He growls and snarls with snapping sounds.
His lizard stride is somewhat gawky
(He's never made it to Milwaukee).

Lumberman Gene Shepard kept one
chained up in his barn
Though some believe his claim was just
a money-making yarn:
To curious tourists in the town
who'd want to sneak a peek
He sold tickets for a dime
and took in half a grand a week.

I is for Igopogo

There's an Igopogo in the lake,
I know because I've seen it.
He swims among the reeds and fish,
You know you best believe it.

He's mostly harmless so they say,
I don't know that I agree.
He ate a sailboat yesterday,
They only found debris.

I wouldn't like to meet him in
A darkened alleyway.
Luckily he seems confined
To waterways and bays.

J is for Jersey Devil

The year was 1735
A normal child was born alive
Its evil side began to thrive—
It's the Jersey Devil!
Before the clergy could arrive
Its growth went into overdrive
It grew wings and took a dive—
It's the Jersey Devil!
Around South Jersey folks would run
From Mother Leeds's 13th son
His evil deeds had just begin—
He's the Jersey Devil!
His horse-like head and cloven feet
The leathery wings he loves to beat
Strike fear in those he's going to meet
He's the Jersey Devil!
Avoid this cursed and airborne beast
His reign of terror has not ceased
Your flesh will be this monster's feast—
He's the Jersey Devil!

K is for Kraken

When sailors in the 18th century
Set their sails and went to sea
The deepest horror that beset them
—any guess what that might be?
Was it lack of wind that made
Their sails and rigging slacken?
Storm clouds blotting out the sun
And making the outlook blacken?
No my friend,
In the end
Their greatest fear was the Kraken.

This giant octopus or squid
With tentacles as long as ships
Giant staring eyes (no eyelid)
Snapping beak instead of lips.
This was a sailor's worst nightmare:
Acephalopod gives the biggest scare.
Next to this, no giant cetacean
Or sharp-clawed outsized red crustacean
No pirate-European or Asian—
Could enter into the equation.

Not scurvy, sunburn, malnutrition
Can interrupt their briny mission
But a Kraken attack
Can send them all back
To their Maker. It feels no contrition.

L is for Loveland Frog

Five feet tall and right behind you
Watch out for the Loveland Frog
The best-known big amphibi-human
To hail from a big western bog.
Is he a giant tailless gecko?
Does he devour feral dogs?
Is he what happens when pollution
Mutates all of Loveland's frogs?
His sticky tongue is poised for an attack
His giant slimy chest is heaving!
Did I mention he's behind you?
And one more thing—I'll just be leaving.

M is for Mothman

All hail, West Virginia's Mothman!
Whose tale is totally goth, man!
A storm raged through town
A bridge just fell down
Through it all,
this strange beast cut a swath, man!

N is for Ningen

At the bottom of the world,
In the icy-cold ocean,
Lives a strange creature,
That's causing quite a commotion.

It's shaped like a human,
But one hundred feet long.
They say it's white as a sheet,
And they couldn't be wrong.

They call it a Ningen,
Named in Japan,
And they say it's been out there,
Since time began.

But there's nothing to fear,
It isn't a threat.
No one's been hurt,
By an old Ningen yet.

O is for Owlman

In the woods in the parish of Mawnan
And up on the church roof and spire
Lurks a dark and mysterious figure
With eyes glowing red like a fire.
Its body is dark with black feathers
Its wings stretch as wide as car
And when it appears,
So do your dark fears
And things seem more bleak than they are.

They call this strange creature the Owlman
As tall as a man on clawed feet
He appears to mostly young women
Before beating a hasty retreat.
He won't hang around or attack you
He doesn't need that to cause you dread
He's ominous, dark, and mysterious
The omens he gives seem so serious
He leaves people pale and delirious
When he shows up, there's trouble ahead.

P is for the Pope Lick Monster

He's a little bit man,
And a little bit goat,
And a little bit sheep.
He lives beneath a bridge
At Pope Lick Creek.

He carries an axe,
To get his revenge.
His origins lie
In an ancient woodhenge

So, stay far away
From that trestle bridge,
Or he'll take you back
To his lair on the ridge.

And then he'll kill you
And hang you,
Deep in the woods,
As a warning to others,
That meeting this monster
Can lead to no good.

Q is for Quetzalcoatl

A snake with feathers? That sounds weird!
His coils and fangs should be revered
His godlike power's not disappeared—
Here comes Quetzalcoatl!
Aztecs say that he's divine
And coils across the whole skyline
Bringing maize on which to dine
Here comes Quetzalcoatl!
A god or monster? You decide!
This feathered serpent shall abide
Central America's joy and pride
Here comes Quetzalcoatl!

R is for Raystown Ray

Raystown Ray is in the lake, they say,
And he's been there for a long long time.
Down at the bottom in the deep deep water
With the relics and the slime.

He's a herbivore and a gentle soul,
But he scares the tourists anyway.
They run from the water with a hoot and a holler
While the locals just swim and play.

Old Raystown Ray is huge, they say.
His body must be sixty feet long.
He swims under water cause he must be shy,
And he knows he just doesn't belong.

There's no place in this world for an old sea monster.
He's a figure from the distant past.
But on a moonlit night when the light's just right,
And the lake is smooth and vast,

You'll still see him swimming from the corner of an eye
He's a legend that's built to last.
Raystown Ray is in that lake to stay,
A monster who won't be outclassed.

S is for Snallygaster

Have you seen the Snallygaster?
On his wings he brings disaster
Flying fast and swooping faster
Faster! Faster! Snallygaster!

When the snallygaster flies
Like a dragon through the skies
Who knows what trouble he'll devise—
He's the snallygaster!
Tentacles squirm upon his head
Grab his victims, squeeze them dead
His gaping maw drips bloody red
He's the snallygaster!

Through fields of hairy golden aster
Teeth as white as alabaster
Comes that bringer of disaster
Faster! Faster! Snallygaster!

T is for Thunderbird

When the big storms come across the great north west,
And the dark clouds cover the skies,
Look for the lightning that tears at the night,
Feel the wind as the thunderbird flies.

The ground quivers when its mighty wings flap,
And the animals all run and hide,
But you've nothing to fear from the thunderbird's flight,
Sit back and enjoy the ride.

U is for Urayuli

In the woods in southern Alaska
Are those tree-trunks I can see?
No...they're clad in fur, they're legs
That belong to a tall Urayuli
Ten feet up, you see his face
With glowing eyes, bright as can be
Matted shaggy fur all over
That great tall Urayuli.
He won't hurt you, even though
His long arms reach below his knee
He won't strike a living soul
That gentle tall Urayuli.

But be warned: If you spook him
Underneath the pale full moon
He'll let out a fearsome scream
Like some dark demented loon.

V is for Veo

On the island of Rinca,
Near Flores and Komodo,
Lives a giant 10-foot creature,
You'll never see in a photo.

They say she's an enormous pangolin,
And she yells out "hoo-hoo-hoo"!
She has scales and fur and a very long tail,
And they say her name is Veo.

She eats termites and ants and the occasional crab,
And she keeps to herself most days,
But once in a while, when the mood strikes her right,
She may just come out to play.

W is for Wendigo

When suddenly the air turns cold
We feel a presence taking hold
So scared we cannot be consoled
It's then we know the Wendigo.
This starving human-eating shade
Smells like something long decayed
And as for us—we feel afraid
When we know the Wendigo.
Fear stabs at us like a knife
As this monster's hungry strife
Makes us see our very life
End in woe. The Wendigo.

X is for Xiao

In the forests of China
Lives a bird called a Xiao,
Which according to sources
Is pronounced like shy-ow.

It's an odd-looking bird,
It has only one eye.
I'm not even sure
It knows how to fly.

The thing has four wings
And a tail like a dog.
It sounds like a magpie,
And it eats like a hog.

So, look out for the Xiao,
If you're deep in those woods.
He's only a bird,
But his intentions are good.

Y is for Yeti

They call him abominable.
His fur is much thicker than wool.
The snow is a-falling,
The Yeti, they call him.
This snowman's phenominable.

Z is for Zaratan

It floats in the ocean with an Island on its back
That looks like a tropical paradise.
Its body lies hidden, it waits to attack,
And somebody will pay the price.

Sailors drop anchor and climb ashore,
At least that is what they believe.
They walk unaware of what they will endure
When Zaratan starts to heave.

The sailors all scream as Zaratan moves.
He takes them under the waves.
When the morning arrives,
There are none that survive,
They're all in a watery grave.

Made in the USA
Middletown, DE
23 April 2023